The Journey to God's Calling

The Journey to God's Calling

(The True Story of a Young Boy's Faith and Transformation from Ghana to America)

Baffour Nkrumah-Appiah (Reverend)

Baffour Nkrumah-Aapiah
The Journey to God's Calling
(The True Story of a Young Boy's Faith and Transformation from Ghana to America)

Published by Spines
ISBN 979-8-89569-858-7

DEDICATED

TO

CALVARY BAPTIST CHURCH, ACCRA, GHANA, FIRST BAPTIST CHURCH OF RANDOLPH, MASSACHUSETTS.

AND

MY FRIENDS DURING THIS JOURNEY

MR.& MRS. AUGUSTUS & COMFORT QUARSHIE

MR. & MRS. EBENEZER & STELLA DEI

THE LATE FRANCIS NKRUMAH- APPIAH

MR. & MRS. SETH & LINDA FIATI

Contents

Introduction

God's call on our lives is one of the most sacred and transforming truths in the Christian journey. It's a call that goes beyond the confines of career choices, geographical locations, and worldly achievements.

In truth, God's calling is not about a specific destination or a fixed plan we can map out. It is, at its heart, about faithfulness—the kind of faithfulness that endures through seasons of uncertainty, struggles, and the unexpected paths life often takes.

The real essence of God's calling is found in how we respond to His presence, His purpose, and His plan for our lives, not in the accolades we gather or the places we go.

This story is one of such a journey. It follows the life of Opie, a young boy from a small village in Ghana, who, through divine guidance and years of wrestling with the call on his life, ultimately discovers the greater purpose behind God's summons.

Like many of us, he struggled with understanding that the ultimate calling was not about pursuing a prestigious career or arriving at a particular place of success but about walking in faithfulness to God's plan, wherever it may lead.

The idea of God's call is woven throughout the Scriptures, reminding us that His ways are often not our ways and His thoughts are higher than our own (Isaiah 55:8-9). When God calls someone, He is not primarily concerned with the specifics of a career or a title.

Rather, His concern is about the heart—the obedience, trust, and faithfulness of the one He calls. "For many are called, but few are chosen" (Matthew 22:14). The "call" is universal, extending to every believer in Christ, but it is not simply about doing something—it is about being someone. It is about being conformed to the image of Christ, fulfilling His purposes through whatever path He lays before us.

The Apostle Paul speaks of this in Romans 8:28-29, when he assures us that "we know that in all things God works for the good of those who love him, who have been called according to his purpose."

The journey may not always make sense at the moment, but God works through every circumstance, good and bad, to shape us into His likeness and accomplish His will. This calling, therefore, is not about a destination, but about purpose. It is about growing in obedience and faithfulness wherever we are, in whatever role or situation God places us.

Opie's story is a reminder that the outward circumstances of our lives—whether we find ourselves in a taxicab, a classroom, a corporate office, or a pulpit—are not the true measure of God's calling. His calling transcends what the world defines as "success." It is rooted in faithfulness to God and trust in His guidance, regardless of how our plans may unfold.

Jesus teaches us that those who are faithful in little will be entrusted with much (Luke 16:10). This is not just a matter of wealth or position; it's about how we steward the moments of life, the opportunities we're given and the gifts we've been entrusted with.

Chapter 1
The First Stirring – A Village in Ghana

Opie's story begins in the serene yet humble village of Kwapong, a small rural settlement nestled between rolling hills in the Brong-Ahafo Region of Ghana. The village was far removed from the hustle of the city, where modern conveniences were scarce, and life moved at a slower pace.

There was peace here, but also poverty. Yet it was within this peaceful, simple environment that the seeds of God's calling were first planted in Opie's heart. His family were devout Christians, and the small church in the village served as both a place of worship and community.

Sundays were special, with a choir that could make the angels sing, and an elderly pastor who spoke with the wisdom of generations. Opie, a curious and earnest young boy, often sat in the pews of the church, watching as people brought their tithes and offerings, their prayers, and their hopes.

After some time, the family moved to Accra, the capital city of Ghana. Opie was recruited to a nearby church conducted in a small makeshift building under a big Oak tree across town, being run by the missionaries of the Southern Baptist Church of the USA.

It was during one of these Sundays, just after the morning service, when Opie found himself alone in the church courtyard, resting under the shade of this large tree.

He had been wrestling with something deep within him—a sense that his life would not be like the others in his city. Though his friends and neighbors seemed content with simple lives, Opie couldn't shake the feeling that he was destined for something greater.

That day, as the congregation hummed quietly around him, Opie heard a voice. It wasn't an audible voice but a whisper in his heart—clear, distinct, and undeniably from God. *"I have called you to be my messenger. I will send you far from here, and your voice will be heard in lands beyond the hills of Accra."*

. . .

Opie didn't fully understand what this meant. How could a simple boy like him, born into humble beginnings, be called to go beyond his simple environment? Yet, that was the beginning. From that moment, something inside him stirred. He felt the weight of it—the weight of a divine calling that was not his to resist.

Chapter 2
A Leap of Faith-The Decision to Leave

As Opie grew, so did his understanding of God's call on his life. He saw his friends and neighbors settle into traditional roles—becoming farmers, fishermen, or tradespeople, even some going into local religious ministries, so It was the way of life for younger people.

But every time he prayed, that whisper would return, reminding him of something greater. God was calling him—not to live as the others lived, but to follow a different path.

The call was so strong that it burned in his heart, and it was all he could think about. He was known in his circles as a young man with a passion for the gospel, a fervor that wasn't typical for boys his age.

It was during one church service that a visiting missionary spoke about the great need for Christian workers in the West, especially in America. Opie's heart burned with a desire to answer the call. "America?

At the age of 16, Opie made the decision that would change the course of his life. He would leave Accra and follow the call to America, a land he had heard about in stories from missionaries who passed through Ghana.

This decision did not come lightly. It meant leaving behind his family, his community, and all that he had ever known. But the call was undeniable. Opie believed that God was sending him to a land far away for a purpose far greater than his own understanding.

His family, though initially hesitant, saw the seriousness in their son's eyes. They knew that God was calling him to something significant. His mother, in particular, had prayed for him daily, trusting that God would reveal His will in His time.

. . .

Though the cost of sending their son to America was immense, both spiritually and financially, they ultimately gave their blessing. With that, Opie packed his bags, said his goodbyes, and left for the unknown world of New York City.

Chapter 3
Arrival in New York City – A City of Dreams and Challenges

In 1978, later in his teens, Opie landed in New York City with little more than a few hundred dollars in his pocket and a heart full of dreams. He had been accepted into a local community college, but the reality of life in a bustling, unfamiliar city soon began to sink in.

The culture shock was intense, and the challenges were numerous. For the first time in his life, he experienced loneliness, frustration, and doubt. The streets of New York, filled with noise, opportunity, and temptation, seemed far removed from the small circle of friends and family and the quiet voice that had once called him.

To make ends meet, Opie took a job driving a yellow taxicab in Manhattan. Long nights and exhausting shifts behind the wheel became his routine. Yet, even amid the hustle and grind of the city, there was a nagging sense of purpose in his heart—something telling him that he had not come to America just to survive but to thrive for a greater reason.

His arrival in New York City was nothing short of overwhelming. The noise, the crowds, the lights—everything was so different from his peaceful life back home. The towering skyscrapers, the rush of people in every direction, and the cultural diversity were things he had only ever seen on television or heard about from others.

Yet amidst all the wonder, there was a deep sense of isolation. He had left behind the familiar for the unfamiliar, and now, more than ever, he felt the weight of God's call upon him.

In the early days, he stayed in a small apartment with other immigrants from Ghana who had already settled in the city. They were kind but busy; each one focused on their work and survival.

He, though grateful for the roof over his head, couldn't ignore the sense of loss that lingered. He felt distant from the God who had called him, as if He were far away in the distant hills of Ghana, rather than in the crowded streets of New York.

Chapter 4

The Struggle – Taxi Driving and Distractions

As indicated earlier in the last chapter, in order to survive, Opie found work as a taxi driver, a job that many immigrants in the city took up to make ends meet. Behind the wheel of his yellow cab, he quickly learned the rhythms of the city.

The streets were alive, always bustling, always in motion. He picked up passengers from all walks of life—businessmen in suits, tourists with heavy accents, homeless people seeking a ride across town, and families with children going to the airport. Each person brought their own story, their own struggles, and sometimes, their own questions about life and faith.

. . .

But the work was exhausting. Each day was filled with long hours on the road, navigating through traffic, picking up fares, and fighting exhaustion. Though he loved the idea of making a difference in people's lives, he began to feel disconnected from his original purpose.

The streets of New York were far removed from the mission field he had imagined. He began to wonder if the call he had heard as a boy was just a fantasy, a youthful ideal that had no place in the real world.

As the months turned into years, he grew increasingly disillusioned. He had come to America with high hopes, but now, he was caught in the daily grind of survival. It was a far cry from the life he had imagined when he first left Ghana.

And again, as years passed, the allure of the city's excitement and wealth began to pull Opie further away from the path he thought God had called him to. The nights spent driving the taxi turned into a blur of faces, noise, and fleeting encounters with strangers.

He began to fall into the rhythm of life in the city, a rhythm that was not conducive to his faith. The distractions of a busy life, combined with the challenges of living in a foreign land, led him to question whether God's calling was even real.

In the quiet moments, however, he would still remember that moment under the shades of the big Oak tree, and the promise of God to guide him. But it was hard. The weight of the city, the overwhelming demands of work, and the lack of community made it difficult for him to focus on anything beyond survival.

Chapter 5
The Turning Point – A Crisis of Faith, Doubts and Longing for Purpose

The turning point in Opie's journey came one fateful night, after a long shift driving his taxi. He had just dropped off a passenger in the heart of Manhattan when he pulled over to the side of the road, tired and defeated.

He realized that he was running from God's call, burying it beneath the distractions of life. The crisis forced him to confront his faith head-on, and for the first time in years, he began to seek God earnestly once more.

As he sat in the driver's seat, a deep sense of emptiness washed over him. His life felt like a never-ending cycle of work, sleep, and more work. He had drifted so far from the call he had once felt so strongly.

. . .

In that moment of deep frustration, he cried out to God. *"God, where are you? Why have you brought me here? What am I supposed to do now?"*

It was then that the answer came—not in a booming voice, but in a quiet whisper, just as it had so many years ago under the baobab tree.

"You are here because I have a purpose for you. It's not about the job you do or the place you live. It's about faithfulness to My call. Stay faithful, and you will see what I have for you."

He felt the weight of those words. His eyes filled with tears, not out of sadness but out of a deep sense of reassurance. God was still with him.

The journey was far from over. He knew then that he had not come to America to chase fame, fortune, or success.

He had come to live out the call of God—to be faithful in whatever place he found himself, whether in a taxi or behind a pulpit.

Chapter 6
A New Direction – The Path to Ministry

By 1983, Opie had enrolled in a local college to study economics and finance. He found that education was not just an opportunity for self-improvement but a way to prepare himself for something greater.

His academic journey brought new friendships, mentorship, and spiritual growth. He began attending a local church where the congregation embraced him like family. His newfound faith community gave him a sense of belonging and helped him reconnect with the dream of ministry that had once felt so distant.

While studying, he also became involved in the church's outreach programs. He found that helping others, sharing the gospel, and serving the community gave him a deep sense of fulfilment.

It was in those moments, serving in small ways, that he began to realize the true nature of his calling—he was not meant to be a missionary in the way he had originally imagined, but a missionary in his own unique context here in America.

The next few years were marked by significant change in Opie's life. He returned to church with renewed vigor and began attending Bible studies again.

He reached out to the local Ghanaian community in New York and the surrounding cities, and through that network, he found a mentor—a pastor friend from Ghana who resides in Boston, Massachusetts, who had been serving in the city for many years.

Under the pastor friend's guidance, he rediscovered his passion for ministry and began to serve in small ways, helping with outreach programs and being actively involved in student afternoon fellowships in the Bronx with other Ghanaian student expatriates.

. . .

His heart burned with a desire to serve God and share the love of Christ with others. He realized that his true calling was not to live for himself or for the comforts of this world, but to live in service to God and others.

It was then that he decided to leave his job as a taxi driver and pursue a path of full-time ministry. His decision wasn't easy. It meant stepping away from the comfort of friends and the student fellowships that have shielded him from the New York City lifestyle he was walking away from. In short, he knew that God had called him to something far greater.

Chapter 7
The Corporate Ladder – A New Direction

After graduating from Fordham University in New York, despite the years of struggle and growth, he knew that there was more ahead of him. God had called him to serve, and now he was ready to live out that calling in a new chapter.

Leaving behind his friends and church family in New York was difficult, but he was eager to embrace the new opportunity to grow and serve. Upon his arrival in Boston, Opie was struck by the city's blend of old-world charm and new-world ambition.

The history of the city was palpable, and it was clear that God had planted him here for a reason. Boston was known for its rich history in education, culture, and faith, but it also had its challenges.

The church he joined was a melting pot of individuals from different racial, cultural, and socioeconomic backgrounds, and he knew that his experience as an immigrant would help him connect with the diverse congregations.

His life took another unexpected turn. He was offered a position at a major bank in Boston, a role that would open the door to financial stability and security.

At first, he hesitated, but the thought of providing for his family back home and the family he anticipates having here in America, as well as the prestige that came with the job, persuaded him to take the leap.

He climbed the corporate ladder quickly, becoming a bank manager by the early 1990s. The job came with impressive perks—high salary, benefits, and status—but it also brought new challenges.

The deeper he got into the corporate world, the more he began to feel the tug of something missing. His work, while important, seemed to lack the fulfilment he had once hoped for. Despite his outward success, He felt like he was slowly losing touch with the true call God had placed on his life once again.

Chapter 8
A Reawakening – God's Voice Again

Later that fall, while attending a church retreat, he experienced another breakthrough. During a prayer session, he felt the same stirring in his heart that he had felt as a young boy in Ghana.

God was reminding him again about the calling—not just to be a banker or a businessman, but to lead and serve in the ministry. He wept as he felt the weight of God's call on his life. He had spent so many years drifting, but now he knew it was time to return to what he had been created for.

At that moment, he made a decision. He would step away from his corporate career and devote himself fully to God's service. The next chapter of his journey was about to begin, and he was finally ready to embrace it.

. . .

In the early 2000's, he enrolled in seminary at Gordon-Conwell Seminary in Boston Massachusetts, leaving behind his lucrative career in banking. It was a huge step of faith—one that his friends and colleagues could not understand.

But for Opie, the choice was clear. He began preparing to serve as a missionary, not in the foreign lands he had once envisioned, but right here in America, where he felt God had called him to make an impact.

Through seminary, he deepened his understanding of Scripture, theology, and ministry. He learned how to preach, how to lead, and how to shepherd God's people. It was a challenging but rewarding period of growth and transformation.

After graduation, Opie was ordained as an Associate Pastor and began serving in a local church. His ministry was marked by a unique combination of cultural understanding, deep faith, and an unshakable commitment to God's calling.

He reached out to immigrants, to the lost and broken, and to anyone who had lost sight of God's purpose for their lives. Opie's story is one of incredible transformation—not just for him, but for everyone whose life he touched.

Through struggles and doubts, through moments of deep pain and confusion, he had finally answered the call. And as he stood before his congregation, preaching the gospel with passion and clarity, he knew one thing for certain: he had found his true purpose, not in what he did, but in who he had become through faithfulness to God's call.

Chapter 9
Meeting Sarah – A Divine Appointment

It was in Boston that Opie's life took another unexpected turn—this time in the form of a woman named Sarah. He had been serving faithfully in the church his pastor friend introduced him into for a few months when one Sunday, after the morning service, a young woman approached him with a warm smile.

Sarah was a healthcare professional who had recently relocated to Boston from her original country of St. Lucia. She had been attending the church with a friend and was immediately drawn to the vibrant worship and the clear passion in Opie's pastor friend's preaching.

She had heard about his journey from Ghana to New York City and to Boston, and she felt an inexplicable connection to his story. He had often focused so much on his ministry and the work before him that he hadn't thought much about his personal life.

But when Sarah introduced herself, he felt a stirring in his heart. There was something special about her—a quiet strength and a deep love for people, qualities that mirrored his own. She was kind, humble, and had an undeniable warmth that made everyone around her feel comfortable.

Over the next few months, Opie and Sarah grew closer. They found they shared many interests, from a love of gospel music and the arts to their deep commitment to serving God. He was drawn to Sarah's heart for the marginalized in society as she worked tirelessly with children in low-income communities.

As they spent more time together, they began to talk about their dreams and aspirations, and it quickly became clear to both of them that God had brought them together.

One afternoon, as they sat around a swimming pool in the backyard of the pastor friend's house, Opie looked into Sarah's eyes and said, "I believe God has brought us together for a purpose. I want to walk alongside you as we both serve Him."

Sarah smiled, her eyes glistening. "I feel the same way," she replied. "I think God has something beautiful in store for us."

Chapter 10
A New Family – Blessings Beyond Measure

Sometime later that year, Opie and Sarah were married in a simple yet beautiful ceremony, surrounded by family, friends, and members of the church they both served. It was a day of joy and celebration, a culmination of years of preparation and prayer.

The love that they had for each other reflected the love they both had for God, and together, they were ready to face the future. The following year, their first child, a son named Michael, was born. The arrival of their son filled their home with joy and laughter, and he found his heart overflowing with love.

He had longed to be a father, and now, with Michael in his arms, he could see how God's plan for his life was unfolding in beautiful ways. A few years later, another son, Joseph, was born, completing their family.

Sarah and Opie, as parents, were committed to raising their children with strong Christian values, ensuring that they understood the importance of faith, service, and love for others.

As his family grew, so did his responsibilities. He continued to serve as an executive pastor in his church, guiding the congregation through difficult seasons, providing counsel, and preaching the gospel with integrity.

But he also felt an increasing sense of responsibility to the wider community of churches in the area. He had always believed that the body of Christ was meant to work together, and this conviction was growing stronger with each passing year.

Chapter 11

The Missionary Heart – A Global Perspective

Even as Opie focused on his local ministry, he never lost sight of his broader calling. He started organizing mission trips back to Ghana, bringing others from his church to witness the needs and opportunities in his home country; however, he also realized the need to invest more in the country that has given him so much.

Becoming a Moderator

In the middle 2000's, after several years of faithful service in his church, Opie received a call that would alter the trajectory of his ministry. The Old Colony Baptist Association (OCBA), a network of 49 churches in Massachusetts, was in need of a new moderator.

. . .

The association had been struggling with division and disunity, and the leaders were searching for someone who could bring a fresh vision and a spirit of unity to the organization.

Opie was asked to consider taking on the role of moderator. It was a significant position, requiring someone with experience in leadership, a deep understanding of church dynamics, and a heart for reconciliation and renewal.

Though he had always been content serving in his local church, he felt God's call to step up and accept the role. It was clear that this was an opportunity for him to serve not only his own congregation but also the wider body of Christ in Massachusetts.

Becoming the moderator of the OCBA was both an honor and a challenge. His first few months in office were marked by long meetings, difficult decisions, and the need for sensitive diplomacy.

The churches within the association were diverse in many ways—racially, socioeconomically, and theologically. However, Opie believed that despite these differences, the churches shared a common mission: to spread the love of Christ and advance His kingdom.

. . .

He set out to unite the churches under a shared vision of love, service, and mutual respect. He hosted several conferences where pastors from different congregations could meet, share experiences, and pray together.

He also focused on outreach, encouraging the churches to work together on community service projects and missions both locally and abroad. His leadership was rooted in humility and the belief that unity in Christ was stronger than any division.

During his time as moderator, the OCBA grew in its sense of unity and purpose. The churches were working together more effectively, and Opie's influence extended beyond the walls of his own congregation.

He was often invited to speak at conferences, church gatherings, and denominational meetings, where his message of hope and reconciliation resonated with many.

He has also begun supporting missions in other parts of Africa and beyond, knowing that his life had been touched by global experiences and that he was now in a position to help others discover the love of Christ.

Chapter 12
Personal Reflection on the Past

As Opie looked back on his journey, he could see how God had woven each part of his life together. From the village in Ghana to the streets of New York, from taxi driving to corporate success, and now to full-time ministry, each step had shaped him into the man and the theologian he had become.

It wasn't always easy, and there were many moments of doubt and struggle, but he had come to understand that his life had a purpose—a divine purpose that only became clearer with time.

Again, he realizes that looking back is not just a matter of recounting events—it's about seeing how far he has come, how much he has grown, and how God has shaped his life in ways he never could have imagined.

There were times when he felt lost, uncertain, and overwhelmed by the magnitude of the calling he believed God had placed on his life. But as he looks back now, with the perspective of time, he can see that every step, every struggle, and every moment of doubt was a vital part of the process.

When he first began writing this journey, he was still grappling with the idea of what it meant to be called by God. He thought that a "calling" was something grand and clear-cut.

A moment of divine intervention, where everything would suddenly fall into place, and he would know exactly what he was supposed to do with his life. What he didn't realize, and what he now understands so much more clearly, is that God's call is rarely as straightforward as we hope.

Instead, it unfolds over time, and it often looks much different than we expect.

He remembers the early chapters of this book, where he was deeply wrestling with questions like, *What is his purpose? Why has he been placed on this earth?* These questions haunted him, especially when he was younger.

. . .

He knew that God had a plan for his life, but he couldn't see it. There were moments when he felt like he was walking through life blindfolded, stumbling from one decision to the next, never quite sure if he was on the right path. He often felt like he was missing some vital piece of the puzzle —like everyone else had figured it out except for him.

Looking back now, he can see that this uncertainty was part of God's design. He wasn't hiding His will from him, but instead, He was inviting him into a deeper relationship with Him. That relationship, he now understands, isn't about having all the answers.

It's about trust. Trusting that God has a plan, even when he can't see it. Trusting that His timing is perfect, even when he wants to rush ahead. And trust is something he had to learn over time, sometimes the hard way.

God was never about our own abilities or strengths. It was about our willingness to surrender and trust that He would provide what we needed when the time came.

Looking back, he sees how crucial that moment was. He had to let go of his need to control everything.

. . .

He had to stop striving so hard to make things happen on his own and instead learn to walk in faith, step by step. The process of surrendering to God's call is ongoing, and it's something he still struggles with at times, but he is much more at peace with it now. He understands that surrender isn't about giving up—it's about giving in to God's greater plan for my life.

The other thing he has come to appreciate over time is the role of community in discerning God's call. In the early chapters, he was very much focused on his individual journey. He believed that his calling was something he had to figure out on his own.

But as he progressed in his journey, he came to see that God uses others to help guide us. He had to learn to listen—not just to God, but to the people He placed around him.

He remembers how his best friend, Augustus, had helped him realize this.

He was having one of their long conversations about life and faith, and he said something that really stuck with him: *"Opie, you're not supposed to do this alone. God has placed people in your life to help you discern His will".*

That conversation was a wake-up call. He had been so focused on his personal struggles that he failed to see the importance of the community around him. He now understands that our callings are not isolated.

We are all connected, and God often speaks to us through the wisdom, encouragement, and challenges of others. Looking back on this journey, he can see how much God has taught him about trust, patience, humility, and community.

The process has been much slower and more complex than he imagined, but it has also been more beautiful than he could have ever predicted. God has been so faithful to him—guiding, shaping, and refining him every step of the way. And even when he couldn't see it, he now knows that He was with him, leading him toward the purpose He had designed for him from the very beginning.

As he continues on this journey, he no longer feels the same urgency or pressure to have everything figured out. He understands now that the calling he has received is not a destination but a lifelong journey of becoming the person God has created him to be.

It's not always easy, and there are still days when he feels uncertain, but he is no longer afraid of the unknown.

Because he knows that God is with him and that His call will continue to unfold in his life.

Chapter 13
A Life of Fulfillment – Teaching Others to Answer God's Call

As the years passed, Opie's influence continued to grow. He remained faithful to his calling, balancing his roles as a pastor, husband, father, and moderator with grace and integrity.

His heart for God and His people never wavered, and he continued to preach with passion, lead with humility, and serve with a deep sense of purpose.

Opie's story is one of faithfulness to God's call, from the small village in Ghana to the bustling streets of New York and finally to the vibrant city of Boston.

Along the way, he encountered challenges, doubts, and moments of struggle, but through it all, he remained committed to the call God had placed on his life. As a pastor, father, husband, and leader, his life was a testament to God's faithfulness and the power of saying "yes" to His call.

Looking back, Opie knew that the journey wasn't about the specific places he had been or the titles he had earned. It was about being faithful in whatever season God had placed him, trusting that He would guide him every step of the way.

And as he stood before the people he had served for so many years, he could honestly say that the journey—though not always easy—had been worth every step.

As his ministry grew, Opie began to mentor young people who were facing similar struggles. He helped them navigate the tension between their faith and their ambitions, encouraging them to listen to God's voice and remain faithful to the call, no matter how difficult the journey might seem.

Chapter 14
A Legacy of Faith

Today, Opie is a respected pastor and leader, known for his deep faith, humility, and commitment to God's calling. He often shares his story with others, encouraging them to trust in God's plan, even when the path is unclear. His life is a testimony of God's faithfulness and guidance.

Looking back, he sees that much of his understanding of God's call has been influenced by the legacy of faith that has been handed down to him. Many years ago, again, he wrote about his late friend Pastor Francis, a man who lived his life with an unwavering commitment to God.

He wasn't a man of many words, but his life spoke volumes. He didn't leave behind great material wealth or tangible accomplishments that the world would consider significant. Instead, he left behind something far greater: a legacy of quiet, steadfast faith.

As he recounts, he remembers him as a man of full jacket of spiritual formation—praying without ceasing, reading his Bible with devotion, and always serving others, whether it was helping a neighbor with their garden or offering guidance to someone in need.

His faith wasn't flashy, but it was deeply rooted in the knowledge that God had called him to live out His love in the simplest of ways.

That legacy, Opie now realizes, has been the foundation of his own understanding of what it means to follow God's call and have a deeper relationship with Him. It's not always about grand gestures or world-changing actions. Often, it's about being faithful in the small, everyday moments.

When he thinks about the "Legacy of Faith," he also thinks about his parents, especially his mother. Growing up, their faith was not something they preached to him but something they lived. He remembers his mother's quiet prayers at night, and her deep, unwavering belief that God was with us even in our struggles.

He saw how they handled adversity—without complaining, without losing faith, and always trusting in God's provision. Their example taught him that following God's call is not about avoiding challenges, but about trusting Him through the difficulties and believing that He is at work even when things seem unclear.

In the "Legacy of Faith" section, His reflection on the significance of the spiritual mentors who have walked with him over the years is well noted. The late Pastor Francis; he was a model of what it meant to live out a life of faith, even when circumstances were difficult.

To the loss of the Christian community of Boston, Kenya, and other parts of the African Emerging Young Leaders community, the Lord brought him home during one of his African missionary journeys in a plane crash in the waters of the Ivory Coast.

Chapter 15
The Journey Continues

Opie's journey has never been a straight line, but he knows now that God's calling on his life was never about a specific career or destination—it was about faithfulness, obedience, and service.

As he continues to preach and lead, he remains firmly rooted in the belief that his life has always been a mission, one that he will never abandon. Looking forward, he is committed to finishing the race with faith and joy, knowing that God's purposes for him are far greater than anything he could have imagined when he first heard the call under the big shades of the Oak tree at the Akasanoma road in Accra, Ghana all those years ago.

Conclusion: (Food for thought)

In the Old Testament, the story of Samuel's calling (1 Samuel 3:1-10) beautifully illustrates that God's call is often unexpected and arises in the quiet, unnoticed moments of our lives.

Samuel did not know God's voice at first, but through persistence and faithfulness, he learned to hear and respond. The call of God is much like that—a whisper in the quiet moments, a tug in the heart that beckons us forward. And when we finally respond, it is not simply about a task—it is about the transformation that occurs as we align our hearts with His.

This journey of faithfulness, though challenging, is one that never abandons us. As the Apostle Paul declares in Philippians 1:6, "Being confident of this, that He who began a good work in you will carry it on to completion until the day of Christ Jesus."

God is not finished with us. He is working in us, through us, and for us, even when we fail to see the end of the journey. It is in this faithful journey, in saying "yes" to His call each day, that we discover the deeper purpose and significance of our lives.

As you read the story of Opie's life—from the streets of Ghana to the streets of New York City, from taxi driving to banking, and ultimately into full-time ministry—remember this truth: God's call on our lives is not about finding a perfect career or a predetermined destination. It's about saying "yes" to His purpose, wherever we are, and being faithful to walk in His ways, knowing that He is working in us and through us, regardless of the path we walk. Faithfulness to God's calling is the true measure of success in His Kingdom.

God's call, then, is a lifelong journey—one of deepening trust, greater obedience, and an ever-growing understanding of His purposes. It's a journey that never ends because it's a journey into His heart. And in that journey, we find our true calling: to be faithful, no matter where we are, no matter what we're doing, until He calls us home.

About the Author

Reverend Baffour Nkrumah-Appiah is currently the Senior Pastor at First Baptist Church of Randolph, Massachusetts, where he oversees a dynamic ministry of a congregation that is fully engaged in the Kingdom work. A church with a mission to fulfil the Apostle Paul's directive in 1 Corinthians 15: 58, which serves as a reminder that every act of service, no matter how small, contributes to a greater divine purpose. Our church members are encouraged to view their work through an eternal perspective, where their labor in the Lord is seen as part of a grander scheme that transcends temporal concerns.

About the Author

Purpose for writing the book

One of the central themes of the book is the idea that God's calling is not always immediate or easily understood. The author portrays a journey that involves periods of uncertainty, waiting, and even doubt. The calling from God doesn't always come with a loud proclamation or a sudden, dramatic moment of clarity. Instead, it is often revealed gradually, with small nudges that guide a person toward their purpose. This theme speaks to the reality that walking in faith often requires patience and trust—trust that God knows the path ahead, even when we cannot see it clearly.

The process of discernment is another key aspect of the journey. As the author reflects on their own experiences, they come to realize that discerning God's calling is not a solitary pursuit. It involves seeking counsel, listening to mentors, and being open to the voices of the broader community. This reflects the biblical principle that the body of Christ is meant to work together, with each member contributing to the larger purpose God has for His people. The author's recognition that God's voice often comes through others highlights the importance of community in our spiritual journeys. We are not meant to walk alone, and often, it is through relationships that God's will is more clearly revealed.

A significant part of the journey is coming to terms with one's own limitations and fears. Many of the struggles the author faces are internal questions of worthiness, fear of failure, and doubts about one's ability to fulfil God's call. This is a universal experience for many believers, and the author's honest confrontation of these fears serves as both a testament to the struggle and an encouragement to others. The journey to God's calling involves wrestling with these insecurities and ultimately learning to trust that God equips those He calls. The realization that God's call is not based on personal strength or ability but on His faithfulness is a major turning point in the narrative.

The legacy of faith is another important theme that runs throughout the book. The author reflects on the spiritual heritage passed down through generations and acknowledges the powerful influence of family, mentors, and the community in shaping their understanding of God's call.

Purpose for writing the book

This book emphasizes that the journey to God's calling is ongoing and dynamic. It is not a one-time event or decision but a lifelong process of transformation. The call to follow God is not simply about arriving at a destination but about continually growing into the person God has created us to be. The narrative highlights the importance of daily surrender, trust, and obedience as essential components of walking in God's calling. The author's journey serves as a reminder that God's call often involves both action and waiting, both steps forward and moments of rest, but through it all, God remains faithful, guiding each step along the way.

In conclusion, Journey to God's Calling offers valuable insights into the complexities of spiritual growth and the process of discerning and living out God's call. It underscores the need for patience, community, and trust as essential elements of the journey. The narrative encourages readers to embrace the unfolding nature of God's purpose for their lives, knowing that they are not alone in their pursuit and that God is always present, guiding them toward the fulfilment of His greater plan.

Final Prayer

Let us Pray:

Heavenly Father,

Thank You for the calling You have placed on our lives, even when we may not fully understand it.

Lord, help us to trust in Your timing and Your plan, even when the path seems unclear. Teach us to walk in faith, not by sight, knowing that You are with us every step of the way.

Give us the courage to surrender our own desires and fears, and to embrace the purpose You have designed for us. May Your wisdom guide our decisions, and may Your love empower us to serve others along the way. Lord, we ask for strength in the moments of doubt and peace in the moments of waiting.

Final Prayer

May we grow in patience and humility, trusting that You are faithful to fulfil Your promises in our lives.

And as we walk this journey, may our life be a reflection of Your grace, so that we might pass on the legacy

of faith to those who come after us.

In Jesus' mighty name.

Amen.

www.ingramcontent.com/pod-product-compliance
Lightning Source LLC
LaVergne TN
LVHW010500160826
845677LV00012B/2568